W9-BZI-219

Worshiping with Angels and Archangels

An Introduction to the Divine Service

SCOT A. KINNAMAN

ILLUSTRATED BY ARTHUR KIRCHHOFF

CALLIGRAPHY BY EDWARD Q. LUHMANN

CONCORDIA PUBLISHING HOUSE • SAINT LOUIS

The text of the worship service, printed in violet, is taken from *Lutheran Service Book*, Divine Service I. While the particular elements and sequence included here may not be identical in every case to the liturgy of a specific service, *Worshiping with Angels and Archangels* can be used to communicate the purpose and the meaning of the Divine Service.

Because the Holy Scripture is the basis for the liturgy of the Divine Service, Bible passages appear throughout this book to help the reader explore these sources more fully.

Copyright © 2006 Concordia Publishing House
3558 S. Jefferson Ave., St. Louis, MO 63118-3968
1-800-325-3040 • www.cph.org

Manufactured in the United States of America.

Library of Congress Cataloging-in-Publication Data

With gratitude to Miss Polehna and her students,
whose joy of learning the liturgy instructed me even as
I taught them about worshiping with angels and archangels

To Judy and the children in our life
Christopher Bailey
Stacey Marie
Brianna Nicole
Jacob Scot
Rachel Elizabeth

What Is Worship?

Although much about worship seems similar throughout Christianity, Lutherans have a unique perspective on the question "What is worship?" The Lutheran understanding of worship is expressed in the **Divine Service**.

The Athanasian Creed teaches us that true Christian worship can be recognized in two ways. First, we worship the God who is triune, that is, Father, Son, and Holy Spirit. The second way we recognize Christian worship is that it is centered on Jesus Christ, the only-begotten Son of God. Our worship is "divine" because it is Christ-centered.

The Lutheran Confessions teach us about the "service" of the Divine Service: "So the worship and divine service of the Gospel is to receive gifts from God" (Apology of the Augsburg Confession, Article V, paragraph 189). In the Divine Service, God, who calls, gathers, and enlightens the whole Christian Church on earth, comes to serve us with His gracious gifts of Word and Sacrament.

People often think that worship is about what we do for or toward God. The reality is quite different. In the Divine Service, God is providing His service for us. In the reading, the preaching, and the proclamation of His Word and in His Sacraments of Holy Baptism and Holy Communion, God comes to us. In worship, God gives His grace and then we respond with thanks and praise.

Our Lord is the Lord who serves. Jesus Christ came into the flesh not to be served, but to serve and to give His life as a ransom for many. On the cross He offered Himself as a spotless sacrifice for the sin of the whole world. . . . Our Lord serves us today through His holy Word and Sacraments. Through these means He comes among us to deliver His forgiveness and salvation, freeing us from our sins and strengthening us for service to one another and to the world. . . . Having been called, gathered, enlightened, and sanctified by the Holy Spirit, we receive His gifts with thankfulness and praise. With psalms, hymns, and spiritual songs we joyfully confess all that God has done for us, declaring the praises of Him who called us out of darkness into His marvelous light.

Lutheran Service Book, page viii

The Divine Service

The Lutheran Church has retained a historic order for the Divine Service. We follow this order not because we believe it is the only right way but because we believe this ancient pattern of worship most clearly and beautifully serves the purpose of the Divine Service, which is to deliver the gracious gifts of God.

The Divine Service uses two distinct elements that create a framework for our worship each time we gather together. Those parts of the liturgy that do not change each week are called the Ordinary because they are ordinarily present each week in the Divine Service. The Ordinary reflects the changeless and timeless texts of the liturgy, some of which have been in continuous use for more than 1,500 years. The second element of our worship consists of the changeable texts, known as the Propers. The Propers bring variety as they follow the seasons of the Church Year and the associated Scripture readings. The Propers carry the message or theme for the day, which is often taken from the Holy Gospel.

Directions are included as part of the service. These directions are called **rubrics**. Following the rubrics gives us a better idea of what we are to do next.

RUBRIC: Latin for "red"; instructions for conducting the service, often written in red.

One of the first rubrics in the liturgy directs the congregation to experience Silence for reflection on God's Word and for self-examination. Everyone knows what silence is, but few are comfortable with it. This rubric in effect says: "Stop and examine your life according to God's Word." This is the time to bring to mind the sins you have committed this week and lay them before the Lord in the Confession of Sins that follows.

> *Come now, let us reason together,* says the LORD:
> *though your sins are like scarlet, they shall be as white as snow;*
> *though they are red like crimson, they shall become like wool.*
>
> ISAIAH 1:18

For us who stand before God as His baptized and redeemed children, this is not a fearful silence, but a time to remember our fallen, sinful nature and examine our actions in light of the Ten Commandments. It is also a time to reflect on our total dependence on God's mercy for our salvation. Observe the time of Silence for reflection on God's Word and for self-examination, and then be ready to hear His freeing Word and Absolution, forgiving you for all your sins.

the Preparation

The Preparation has not always been part of the Divine Service. Yet Confession and Absolution have always been seen as proper preparation for those who desire to participate in Holy Communion. The Preparation may be omitted entirely, as it is when we celebrate Holy Baptism immediately after the Hymn of Invocation.

Invocation

In the name of the Father and of the ✝ Son and of the Holy Spirit.
Amen.   *Matthew 28:19b; [18:20]*

The Divine Service begins with the name of God. Invoking His name orders our worship, making it clear that this is His service to us, not our service or someone else's. We call upon God to bless that which will be done in His name.

INVOCATION: From the Latin for "call upon."

We don't come before God on the basis of our merits or by our deeds. We come because, with the whole Church, our Lord has called, gathered, and enlightened us by His Holy Spirit to worship Him. In the **Invocation** we call upon God to be true to His Word, for where His name is, there He has promised to be.

> *For where two or three are gathered in My name, there am I among them.*
>
> MATTHEW 18:20

Here, at the beginning of the service, the Invocation also recalls us to our own baptismal beginning. In Baptism, God's name was placed upon us in the Word and along with the water. The sign of

the cross, first made on our head and on our heart during our Baptism, is now made at the Invocation, reminding us who we are and whose we are in Jesus Christ (Titus 3:5–8).

Confession

As children of the heavenly Father, we are called into His presence in the Divine Service so He can bless us. As we make our appearance before God, Psalm 51 reminds us that we are only beggars, seeking to receive.

Have mercy on me, O God, according to Your steadfast love;
according to Your abundant mercy blot out my transgressions.
Wash me thoroughly from my iniquity, and cleanse me from my sin!
For I know my transgressions, and my sin is ever before me.
Against You, You only, have I sinned and done what is evil in Your sight,
so that You may be justified in Your words and blameless in
Your judgment. . . . Deliver me from bloodguiltiness, O God.

PSALM 51:1–4, 14

In the **Confession**, we are saying "amen," or "yes, yes, this is true," to God's righteous judgment against our sin. But the Lord is present with us and ready to forgive. After all, this is the reason the Lord gathers His people together in the Divine Service, to give them His mercy and grace. "If we confess our sins, He is faithful and just to forgive us our sins and to cleanse us from all unrighteousness" (1 John 1:9).

CONFESSION: The act by which one admits or confesses sin and the guilt of sin.

Confession of Sins

If we say we have no sin, we deceive ourselves, and the truth is not in us. But if we confess our sins, God, who is faithful and just, will forgive our sins and cleanse us from all unrighteousness.

1 John 1:8–9

Silence for reflection on God's Word and for self-examination.

Let us then confess our sins to God our Father.

Most merciful God, we confess that we are by nature sinful and unclean. We have sinned against You in thought, word, and deed, by what we have done and by what we have left undone. We have not loved You with our whole heart; we have not loved our neighbors as ourselves. We justly deserve Your present and eternal punishment. For the sake of Your Son, Jesus Christ, have mercy on us. Forgive us, renew us, and lead us, so that we may delight in Your will and walk in Your ways to the glory of Your holy name. Amen.

I acknowledged my sin to You, and I did not cover
my iniquity; I said, "I will confess my transgressions to the LORD,"
and You forgave the iniquity of my sin.

PSALM 32:5

10

Absolution

[Jesus] breathed on them and said to them, *"Receive the Holy Spirit. If you forgive the sins of anyone, they are forgiven; if you withhold forgiveness from anyone, it is withheld."*

JOHN 20:22–23

Our Lord declares through the mouth of His servant, the pastor, that by His grace and mercy our sins are forgiven. The **Absolution** speaks the Gospel into our ears in a personal way. Through these Gospel words we receive the salvation earned by Christ upon the cross of Calvary; every sin is covered by His blessed death.

Almighty God in His mercy has given His Son to die for you and for His sake forgives you all your sins. As a called and ordained servant of Christ, and by His authority, I therefore forgive you all your sins in the name of the Father and of the ✝ Son and of the Holy Spirit. **Amen.**

ABSOLUTION: The announcement of forgiveness to the penitent sinner.

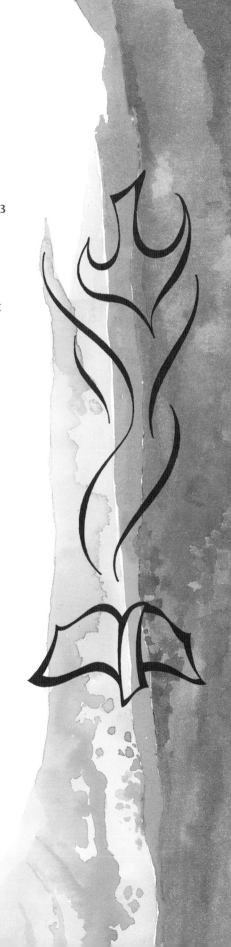

Service of the Word

After the Confession and Absolution, the Divine Service continues with the **Service of the Word**. The purpose of the Service of the Word is to present Christ to the assembled congregation as the people prepare to meet Him in His Supper.

The Service of the Word begins with a song of entrance. This song marks the actual beginning of the Divine Service and the entrance of the pastor to the altar. The altar is the center and symbol of the Lord's presence among His people. There is where the body and the blood of Jesus are distributed under the consecrated bread and wine for the forgiveness of sins. While an Entrance Hymn or Psalm may be sung, a common beginning is to sing the Introit.

Introit

The **Introit**, one of the Propers (the verses chosen are different each Sunday), is sung by the congregation or choir. The Introit is a collection of passages from the Psalms that sets the tone for our worship and introduces the rest of the Divine Service, in which Christ comes to us in His Word and His Sacrament.

INTROIT: Latin for "enter."

13

Kyrie

As we move toward the reading of God's Word, we join with all believers through the ages, in heaven and presently on earth, and ask the Lord for mercy. The **Kyrie** is the first prayer of the gathered congregation. It is a cry for mercy that our Lord and King hear us and help us in our needs and troubles. This prayer is encountered frequently in Scripture, for example, it is used by the Canaanite woman (Matthew 15:22), blind Bartimaeus (Mark 10:46–47), and the ten lepers (Luke 17:12–13).

KYRIE: A shortened form of the Greek words *Kyrie eleison*, which mean "Lord, have mercy."

In peace let us pray to the Lord.
Lord, have mercy.

For the peace from above and for our salvation let us pray to the Lord.
Lord, have mercy.

For the peace of the whole world, for the well-being of the Church of God, and for the unity of all let us pray to the Lord.
Lord, have mercy.

For this holy house and for all who offer here their worship and praise let us pray to the Lord.
Lord, have mercy.

Help, save, comfort, and defend us, gracious Lord.
Amen.

"Jesus, Son of David, have mercy on me!"

MARK 10:47

Hymn of Praise

Confident that the Lord is merciful, we join the whole Church in singing the **Hymn of Praise**. In the traditional Hymn of Praise, the **Gloria in Excelsis**, the pastor begins with the angelic hymn in Luke 2:14: "Glory to God in the highest, and peace to His people on earth." In the Gloria, the Church celebrates Christmas all year long, and we, along with the shepherds, are invited to go and see Jesus in the Scripture readings that follow.

GLORIA IN EXCELSIS: Latin for "glory [to God] in the highest."

Glory to God in the highest, and peace to His people on earth.

Lord God, heavenly king, almighty God and Father: We worship You, we give You thanks, we praise You for Your glory. Lord Jesus Christ, only Son of the Father, Lord God, Lamb of God: You take away the sin of the world; have mercy on us. You are seated at the right hand of the Father; receive our prayer. For You alone are the Holy One, You alone are the Lord, You alone are the Most High, Jesus Christ, with the Holy Spirit, in the glory of God the Father. Amen.   *Luke 2:14; John 1:29*

Christ Jesus . . . is at the right hand of God . . . interceding for us.
ROMANS 8:34

16

The Divine Service also offers a second Hymn of Praise, **"This Is the Feast."** This Easter hymn to the crucified and risen Savior is based on passages from Revelation 5:12–13 and 19:5–9. Because of its resurrection theme, this hymn is used more frequently during the Easter season and on the festivals of Christ celebrated throughout the Church Year.

This is the feast of victory for our God. Alleluia, alleluia, alleluia.

Worthy is Christ, the Lamb who was slain,
whose blood set us free to be people of God.
This is the feast of victory for our God. Alleluia, alleluia, alleluia.

Power, riches, wisdom, and strength,
and honor, blessing, and glory are His.
This is the feast of victory for our God. Alleluia, alleluia, alleluia.

Sing with all the people of God,
and join in the hymn of all creation:
Blessing, honor, glory, and might be to God
and the Lamb forever. Amen.
This is the feast of victory for our God.
Alleluia, alleluia, alleluia.

For the Lamb who was slain
has begun His reign. Alleluia.
This is the feast of victory for our God.
Alleluia, alleluia, alleluia.

Revelation 5:12–13; 19:5–9

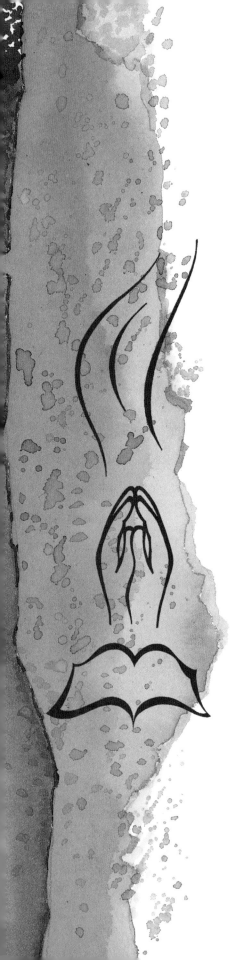

Salutation and Collect of the Day

The Lord be with you.

And also with you. *2 Timothy 4:22*

The **Salutation** is a special greeting between the congregation and its pastor. The Salutation announces the Lord's coming to us in the readings that follow and makes us aware that important things are about to happen.

Let us pray.

The **Collect of the Day** "collects" in a concise and beautiful manner the Gospel message for the day. Most of these prayers have been in continuous use in the Church for more than 1,500 years. In the Collect, we join with the great body of believers, the communion of saints, and with the generations yet to come. The congregation makes the Collect its own with its "amen."

AMEN: The congregation's declaration that what has been said is true and worthy of agreement; "yes, yes, this is most certainly true."

Amen.

Hearing God's Word

The Service of the Word makes a transition from prayer and praise to the hearing of God's Word. The bestowal of God's grace, which was announced in the Introit and prayed for in the Collect, will now take place in the reading and preaching of God's Word. Reading God's Word is the high point for the Service of the Word because wherever God's Word is, there our Lord has promised to be (Matthew 18:20).

Our service follows a simple pattern for the hearing of God's Word with a reading from the Old Testament, one from an apostolic letter (Epistle), and one from a Gospel. In a real sense, the readings from the Old Testament and from an Epistle lead to and find their fulfillment in the Gospel. Origen, an early Christian, called the Holy Gospel the "crown of all Holy Scripture."

> *So faith comes from hearing, and hearing through the word of Christ.*
>
> **ROMANS 10:17**

The words of Holy Scripture are read to "make [us] wise for salvation" (2 Timothy 3:15). They do this by not only telling us about Jesus but also by giving us Jesus, who was crucified for our sins and raised to life for our justification. The Word of God is the Word of life.

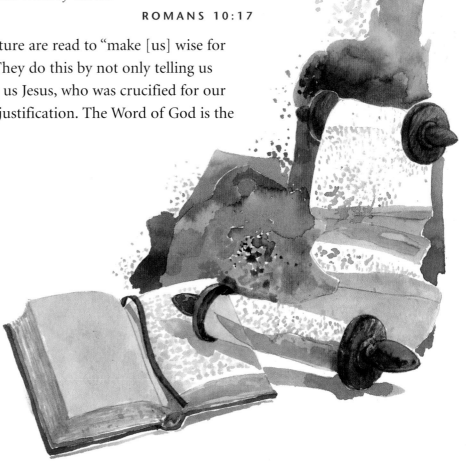

Old Testament Reading and Epistle

The first reading is typically from the Old Testament. Through the history of Israel and the words of the prophets, the **Old Testament Reading** teaches us about God's work in the time before Christ. There we hear the prophecies of the Messiah who would come to men that all people might once again be brought back to God. The Old Testament Reading prepares us to hear the Holy Gospel, which is the fulfillment of the prophecies and promises made in the Old Testament.

This is the Word of the Lord.
Thanks be to God.

Hearing the Word of God, the people respond with words of praise. The **Gradual** is a Proper. It is a portion of a psalm or other Scripture passage that provides a response after the Old Testament Reading.

The **Epistle** gives us God's counsel on how His gracious Word is applied to the hearer and the Church. Often in this reading we hear how God's Word accomplishes what it says—creating faith, bestowing forgiveness, strengthening God's people in their struggles against sin, and enlivening in them the hope of eternal life.

This is the Word of the Lord.
Thanks be to God.

Holy Gospel

Like the Gradual, the **Alleluia and Verse** provide a transition between the readings. The word *alleluia* is Hebrew for "praise the Lord." The Verse prepares us to meet the Christ of God in His Word, hearing of His life, ministry, death, and resurrection for the salvation of all.

Alleluia. Lord, to whom shall we go? You have the words of eternal life. Alleluia, alleluia. *John 6:68*

Simon Peter answered [Jesus], "Lord, to whom shall we go? You have the words of eternal life."

JOHN 6:68

The Holy Gospel according to St. _____, the _____ chapter. **Glory to You, O Lord.**

The **Holy Gospel** always contains the very words or deeds of Jesus. This makes the reading of the Holy Gospel the summit of the Service of the Word, and we recognize this by surrounding our Savior's words with songs of glory and praise and by standing to receive His gracious words.

This is the Gospel of the Lord. **Praise to You, O Christ.**

Hymns and the Hymn of the Day

God's people have been encouraged to sing their prayers, praise, and thanksgiving to God. Why do we sing? Psalm 98 gives us the reason.

> *Oh sing to the* LORD *a new song*
> *for He has done marvelous things!*
> *His right hand and holy arm*
> *have worked salvation for Him.*

PSALM 98:1

The Word of God not only creates faith but teaches us, God's children, His gracious will toward us. God has freely given us His own righteousness. In our hymns we respond to this Good News with singing, reciting back to God the great acts of our salvation in thanksgiving and praise.

Taking cues from Scripture's own songbook, the Psalms, the Church's hymns give us a variety of ways to thank, praise, and proclaim the God who has done all good things for us. In the Divine Service, our singing is related to the readings from Scripture. Hymns enable everyone to join together in proclaiming the scriptural truths read at the lectern, preached from the pulpit, and spoken before the altar.

The **Hymn of the Day** is the principal hymn of the Divine Service and relates to the theme of the day from the Holy Gospel.

Sermon

Our Lord sent His apostles into the world to preach that forgiveness of sins, life, and salvation are found through Him. In the preaching of the **Sermon**, that apostolic Word is proclaimed among us today.

SERMON: The pastor's proclamation, usually based on the Scripture readings for the day.

The Sermon is dependent on all that has gone before it in the Divine Service—the liturgy, the hymns, and the readings. Therefore the message of the Sermon is the fullest expression of the theme of the day. In the Sermon the pastor speaks God's words of judgment and grace to the current situation. In this way, the Sermon also prepares the hearer for the celebration of the Service of the Sacrament. Like the Absolution, the Sermon delivers the forgiveness of sins earned by Christ on the cross. The Divine Service, then, becomes for us grace upon grace (John 1:16).

For the word of the cross is . . . the power of God.
1 CORINTHIANS 1:18

Creed

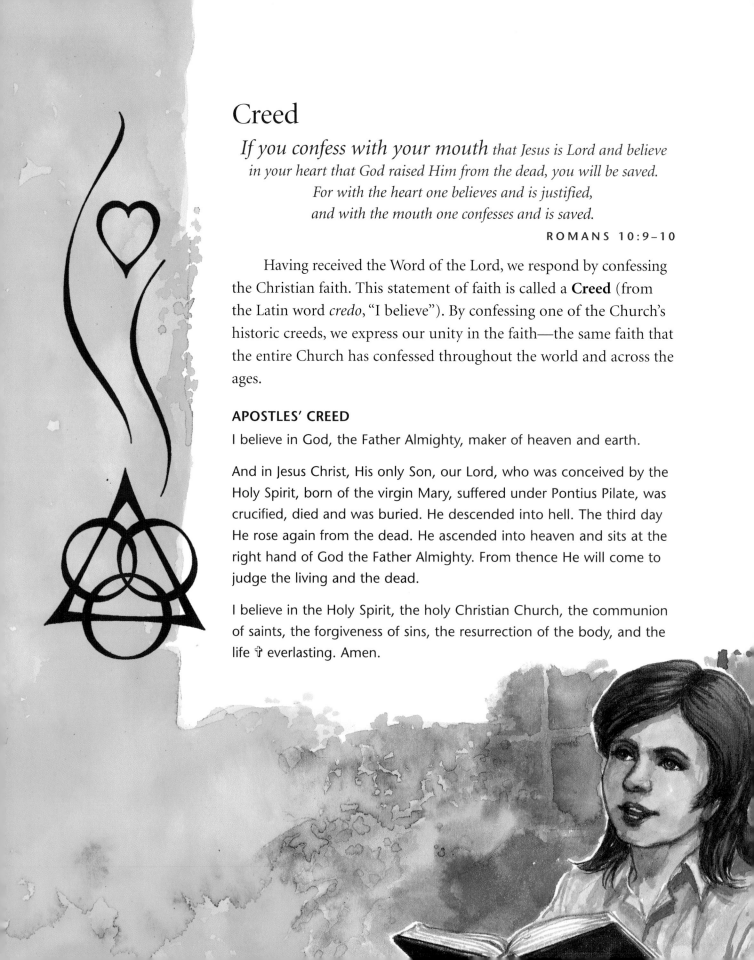

If you confess with your mouth that Jesus is Lord and believe
in your heart that God raised Him from the dead, you will be saved.
For with the heart one believes and is justified,
and with the mouth one confesses and is saved.

ROMANS 10:9–10

Having received the Word of the Lord, we respond by confessing the Christian faith. This statement of faith is called a **Creed** (from the Latin word *credo*, "I believe"). By confessing one of the Church's historic creeds, we express our unity in the faith—the same faith that the entire Church has confessed throughout the world and across the ages.

APOSTLES' CREED

I believe in God, the Father Almighty, maker of heaven and earth.

And in Jesus Christ, His only Son, our Lord, who was conceived by the Holy Spirit, born of the virgin Mary, suffered under Pontius Pilate, was crucified, died and was buried. He descended into hell. The third day He rose again from the dead. He ascended into heaven and sits at the right hand of God the Father Almighty. From thence He will come to judge the living and the dead.

I believe in the Holy Spirit, the holy Christian Church, the communion of saints, the forgiveness of sins, the resurrection of the body, and the life ✝ everlasting. Amen.

There is one body and one Spirit—*just as you were called to the one hope that belongs to your call*—*one Lord, one faith, one baptism, one God and Father of all, who is over all and through all and in all.*

EPHESIANS 4:4–6

NICENE CREED

I believe in one God, the Father Almighty, maker of heaven and earth and of all things visible and invisible.

And in one Lord Jesus Christ, the only-begotten Son of God, begotten of His Father before all worlds, God of God, Light of Light, very God of very God, begotten, not made, being of one substance with the Father, by whom all things were made; who for us men and for our salvation came down from heaven and was incarnate by the Holy Spirit of the virgin Mary and was made man; and was crucified also for us under Pontius Pilate. He suffered and was buried. And the third day He rose again according to the Scriptures and ascended into heaven and sits at the right hand of the Father. And He will come again with glory to judge both the living and the dead, whose kingdom will have no end.

And I believe in the Holy Spirit, the Lord and giver of life, who proceeds from the Father and the Son, who with the Father and the Son together is worshiped and glorified, who spoke by the prophets. And I believe in one holy Christian and apostolic Church, I acknowledge one Baptism for the remission of sins, and I look for the resurrection of the dead and the life ✝ of the world to come. Amen.

Prayer of the Church

First of all, then, I urge that supplications, prayers, intercessions, and thanksgivings be made for all people, for kings and all who are in high positions, that we may lead a peaceful and quiet life, godly and dignified in every way. This is good, and it is pleasing in the sight of God our Savior, who desires all people to be saved and to come to the knowledge of the truth.

1 TIMOTHY 2:1–4

It is both our duty and our privilege as God's children to bring our concerns before Him. In the **Prayer of the Church** we pray not only for our own needs but also for our neighbor. This is seen in the traditional invitation: "Let us pray for the whole people of God in Christ Jesus and for all people according to their needs." This is the longest prayer in the Divine Service and includes petitions

- for the local congregation and the Church at large,
- for right teaching,
- for protection from the assaults of the devil,
- for the government,
- for those who suffer,
- for the welfare and safety of ourselves and others,
- for the conversion of the unbeliever,
- and for the restoration of those who have left the Church.

The Prayer of the Church is the congregation's prayer. All those in the congregation are invited to add their voices to each petition by responding with "Hear my prayer" or with the words from the Kyrie, "Lord, have mercy."

Offering and the Offertory

Just as we respond to the hearing of God's Word in prayer, praise, and thanksgiving, we also respond in the **Offering** by returning to God a portion of the treasure He has given us.

The **Offertory** is sung as the congregation's offering is brought forward and presented before the altar. During the singing of the Offertory, the altar is prepared by the pastor for the celebration of Holy Communion.

The words of the Offertory are from Psalm 116 and join our offering as a sacrifice of praise for all that our Lord has done for us.

What shall I render to the Lord for all His benefits to me? I will offer the sacrifice of thanksgiving and will call on the name of the Lord.
I will take the cup of salvation and will call on the name of the Lord.
I will pay my vows to the Lord now in the presence of all His people, in the courts of the Lord's house, in the midst of you, O Jerusalem.

Psalm 116:12–14, 17, 19

Service of the Sacrament

The **Service of the Sacrament** is the celebration of the Sacrament of the Altar. The Sacrament was instituted by Jesus Christ for the forgiveness of sins. It is to be celebrated by all Christians until Christ comes again on the Last Day.

Because Jesus instituted it, the Sacrament of the Altar is also called the Lord's Supper. In the Service of the Sacrament, those who have been instructed in the faith come to the altar to receive the precious body and blood of Jesus under the forms of bread and wine. Here in the Lord's Supper, Christ comes to be with His holy people and to give forgiveness, life, and salvation.

The cup of blessing that we bless, is it not a participation in the blood of Christ? The bread that we break, is it not a participation in the body of Christ?

1 CORINTHIANS 10:16

Christ's body and blood go into our mouths and into our souls. United with Jesus in this wonderful Sacrament, we are made one not only with Him but also with all Christians throughout the world and with all the saints of heaven. For this reason, the Sacrament is also called Holy Communion.

Preface

The Service of the Sacrament begins with the **Preface**, an ancient dialogue or conversation between the pastor and the people.

The Lord be with you. *2 Timothy 4:22*
And also with you.

Lift up your hearts. *Colossians 3:1*
We lift them to the Lord.

Let us give thanks to the Lord our God. *Psalm 136*
It is right to give Him thanks and praise.

This first part of the Preface is a part of the Ordinary and does not change. It serves as an introduction to the Proper Preface, which changes with each season or festival day of the Church Year. At the close of the Preface, the pastor says, "Therefore with angels and archangels and with all the company of heaven . . ." With these words, we are reminded that our worship is not limited by time or by space. Every time we worship we join the angelic choirs and saints of every age in their ongoing heavenly worship of the Lamb who was slain.

Then I looked, and I heard around the throne . . .
the voice of many angels. . . . And I heard every creature
in heaven and on earth and under the earth and in the sea,
and all that is in them, saying, "To Him who sits on the throne and to
the Lamb be blessing and honor and glory and might forever and ever!"
REVELATION 5:11, 13

Sanctus

As a Hymn of Praise was sung at the beginning of the Service of the Word, so now a song of praise is sung before the Sacrament. The **Sanctus** is the angelic hymn described in the heavenly vision of Isaiah 6. In this vision the seraphim are gathered around the throne of God, proclaiming His holiness and glory.

SANCTUS: Latin for "holy."

By singing this hymn in the Divine Service, the congregation participates in the heavenly chorus. For a time, the division between heaven and earth is gone. Heaven has come down to earth, and all stand together around the throne of almighty God. The confidence that this unseen reality is true comes from faith in Jesus Christ's presence in the Sacrament. In the hosannas of the second half of the Sanctus, we worship Jesus who comes in His Holy Supper (Matthew 21:9).

Holy, holy, holy Lord, God of power and might: Heaven and earth are full of Your glory. Hosanna. Hosanna. Hosanna in the highest. Blessed is He who comes in the name of the Lord. Hosanna in the highest.

Isaiah 6:3; Matthew 21:9

Prayer of Thanksgiving

In the **Prayer of Thanksgiving**, the congregation is led in prayer to thank the Lord for what is about to be received. First, we praise God for the gift of Jesus as the incarnate Son whose death on the cross is the once-for-all sacrifice for the forgiveness of sins. Second, we ask God to deliver what He has promised and that the Spirit would strengthen the faith and prepare the hearts of all those who will receive Holy Communion.

Blessed are You, Lord of heaven and earth, for You have had mercy on those whom You created, and sent Your only-begotten Son into our flesh to bear our sin and be our Savior. With repentant joy we receive the salvation accomplished for us by the all-availing sacrifice of His body and His blood on the cross.

Gathered in the name and the remembrance of Jesus, we beg You, O Lord, to forgive, renew, and strengthen us with Your Word and Spirit. Grant us faithfully to eat His body and drink His blood as He bids us do in His own testament. Gather us together, we pray, from the ends of the earth to celebrate with all the faithful the marriage feast of the Lamb in His kingdom, which has no end. Graciously receive our prayers; deliver and preserve us. To You alone, O Father, be all glory, honor, and worship, with the Son and the Holy Spirit, one God, now and forever.

Amen.

The Words of Our Lord

Sometimes called the *Verba Domini* (Latin for "the words of our Lord"), the pastor speaks **The Words of Our Lord** to consecrate, or set apart, the bread and the wine for God's special use.

Our Lord Jesus Christ, on the night when He was betrayed, took bread, and when He had given thanks, He broke it and gave it to the disciples and said: "Take, eat; this is My ✝ body, which is given for you. This do in remembrance of Me."

In the same way also He took the cup after supper, and when He had given thanks, He gave it to them, saying: "Drink of it, all of you; this cup is the new testament in My ✝ blood, which is shed for you for the forgiveness of sins. This do, as often as you drink it, in remembrance of Me."

Matthew 26:26–28; Mark 14:22–24
Luke 22:19–20; 1 Corinthians 11:23–25

In the Sacrament of the Altar, Christ gives His true body and true blood under the forms of consecrated bread and wine. Once again, God's grace comes to us in the Divine Service. Jesus Himself is present and forgives our sins. This is Good News because Jesus' Word does what it says.

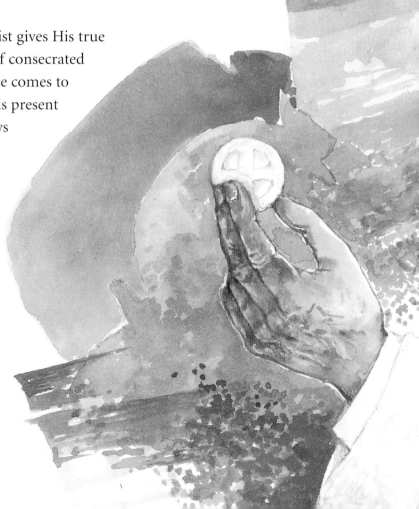

Proclamation of Christ

As often as we eat this bread and drink this cup, we proclaim the Lord's death until He comes. *1 Corinthians 11:26*

Amen. Come, Lord Jesus. *Revelation 22:20*

O Lord Jesus Christ, only Son of the Father, in giving us Your body and blood to eat and to drink, You lead us to remember and confess Your holy cross and passion, Your blessed death, Your rest in the tomb, Your resurrection from the dead, Your ascension into heaven, and Your coming for the final judgment. So remember us in Your kingdom and teach us to pray:

Lord's Prayer

Our Father who art in heaven, hallowed be Thy name, Thy kingdom come, Thy will be done on earth as it is in heaven; give us this day our daily bread; and forgive us our trespasses as we forgive those who trespass against us; and lead us not into temptation, but deliver us from evil. For Thine is the kingdom and the power and the glory forever and ever. Amen.

Matthew 6:9–13

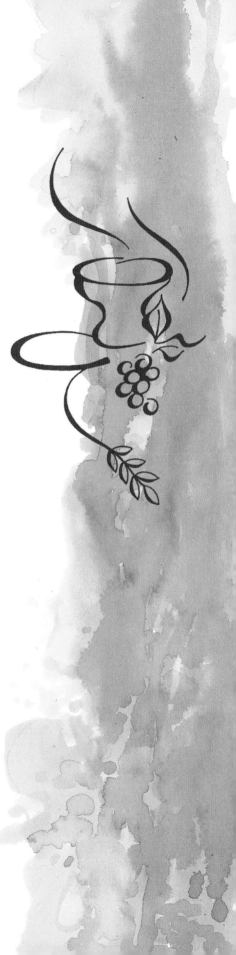

The **Lord's Prayer** is the chief prayer of the Christian Church, and it is prayed here at the chief event of the Divine Service. As children of God, we call upon "our Father" as we prepare to encounter Jesus in His Supper, acknowledging that in the Sacrament He will answer our petitions. The congregation prays, "Thy kingdom come," then receives the kingdom of God in the coming of Christ in His body and blood. We pray, "Thy will be done," then witness salvation being distributed. We pray for forgiveness of sins and hear Christ's own Word proclaiming that in His death He has accomplished everything needed to "forgive us our trespasses."

Pax Domini

PAX DOMINI: Latin for "the peace of the Lord."

The peace of the Lord be with you always.　　　　　*John 20:19*
Amen.

  The pastor holds the body and the blood of Jesus before the congregation and speaks the **Pax Domini** as Christ Himself did on that first Easter when He stood in the midst of His disciples.

> *Jesus came and stood* among them
> and said to them, "Peace be with you."
>
> JOHN 20:19

  The Pax is the voice of the Gospel announcing the remission of sins through its called minister, the pastor. Being at peace with God, those who have been instructed in the faith are called to dine on the Lord's life-giving Supper.

> *Peace to all of you* who are in Christ.
>
> 1 PETER 5:14

Agnus Dei

Standing in the presence of Christ, we sing to Him in the great Communion hymn the **Agnus Dei**.

AGNUS DEI: Latin for "Lamb of God."

John the Baptist foresaw Jesus' death on Calvary, and at Jesus' Baptism, John cried out, "Behold, the Lamb of God, who takes away the sin of the world!" (John 1:29). In Jesus' presence we, too, cry out and sing the praise of Christ, the "Lamb of God," who in His death on Calvary bore our sins, even the sins of the whole world. It is this Christ who has washed us clean by His blood, bringing us His merciful salvation and peace (Revelation 7:14).

Lamb of God, You take away the sin of the world; have mercy on us.
Lamb of God, You take away the sin of the world; have mercy on us.
Lamb of God, You take away the sin of the world; grant us peace.

John 1:29

Take, eat; this is the true body of our Lord and Savior Jesus Christ, given into death for your sins.
Amen.

Take, drink; this is the true blood of our Lord and Savior Jesus Christ, shed for the forgiveness of your sins.
Amen.

Distribution of the Lord's Supper

At the altar, the pastor distributes first the body and then the blood of Jesus. After all have communed, the pastor dismisses those at the altar by making the sign of the cross and saying:

The body and blood of our Lord Jesus Christ strengthen
and preserve you in body and soul to life everlasting.
Depart ✞ in peace.
Amen.

Post-Communion Canticle

At the close of Holy Communion, as the pastor closes the sacred vessels and covers them with a veil, the congregation stands to sing the **Nunc Dimittis**. The Nunc Dimittis is Simeon's prayer of thanksgiving for being allowed to see the Messiah before he died. With the incarnate Christ in his arms, Simeon rejoiced and made his confession (Luke 2:28–32).

NUNC DIMITTIS: Latin for "now let [your servant] depart."

One of the great hymns of Scripture, the use of Simeon's Song as a Post-Communion Canticle is a unique element of Lutheran liturgy. Having seen Christ in the Sacrament—receiving Him in our mouths and so into our souls—we join Simeon in his inspired song.

Lord, now You let Your servant go in peace; Your word has been fulfilled. My own eyes have seen the salvation which You have prepared in the sight of every people: A light to reveal You to the nations and the glory of Your people Israel. Glory be to the Father and to the Son and to the Holy Spirit; as it was in the beginning, is now, and will be forever.
Amen.   *Luke 2:29–32*

Post-Communion Collect

We have received God's good and gracious gifts of Word and Sacrament. However, before we leave and take up our vocations again, we pause and thank God for all that He has done for us.

The **Post-Communion Collect** "collects" our grateful thoughts into one prayer, asking that the gifts received in the Divine Service, and specifically in the Lord's Supper, would strengthen our faith toward God and would carry into our lives and callings as we deal with one another.

Let us pray.

We give thanks to You, almighty God, that You have refreshed us through this salutary gift, and we implore You that of Your mercy You would strengthen us through the same in faith toward You and in fervent love toward one another; through Jesus Christ, Your Son, our Lord, who lives and reigns with You and the Holy Spirit, one God, now and forever.
Amen.

Benediction

In the Old Testament, God gave Aaron and his sons who followed him in the priesthood His very name to use as a blessing for the Israelites (Numbers 6:22–27). So also today in the **Benediction**, the Lord blesses His people with His holy name.

The Lord bless you and keep you.

The Lord make His face shine on you and be gracious to you.

The Lord look upon you with favor and ☩ give you peace.

Amen.

We end the Divine Service as we began—in the name of the Lord and with a threefold speaking of God's holy name. Thus

☩ we depart from God's house with His name upon us;

☩ we depart fed and nourished by Word and Sacrament, having Christ in us;

☩ we go in peace and with God's blessing.

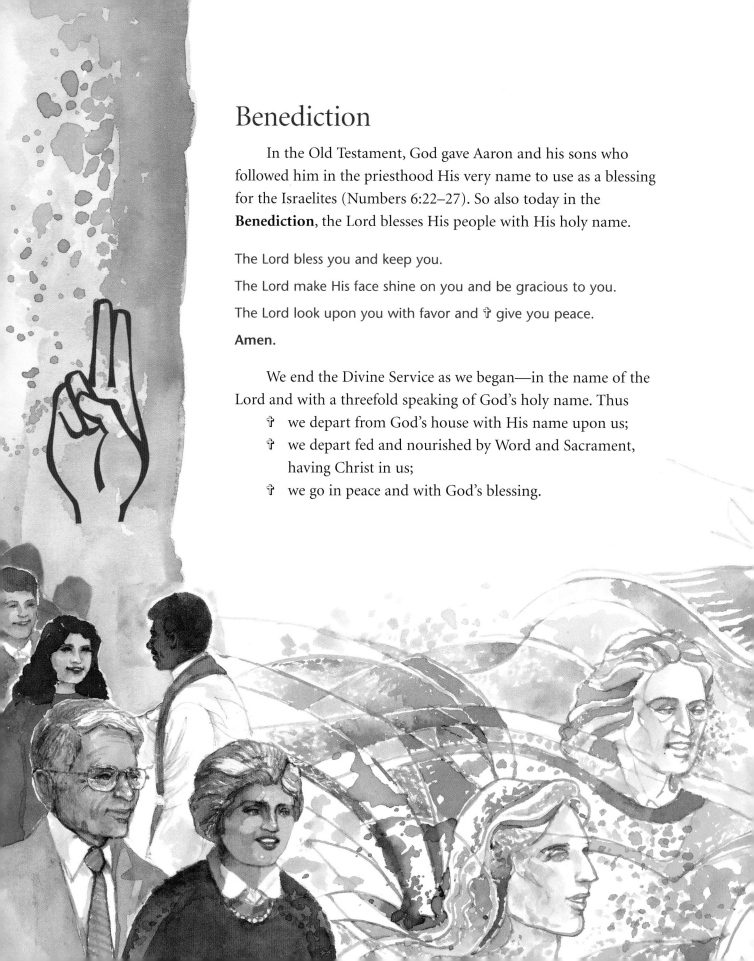

Worshiping with angels and archangels and all the company of heaven—that is our great privilege as the children of God. In the Divine Service, we come before God with nothing to offer but the magnitude of our sin. But out of His great love for us, by the sacrifice of His only Son, the Lamb of God, we do not receive what we deserve. Instead, God grants us His gifts and gives us blessing upon blessing.

Forgiveness. Life. Salvation. These are the gifts given by the Holy Spirit, who calls, gathers, and enlightens the whole Christian Church on earth. These are the gifts given abundantly in the Divine Service—in the Absolution, in the Word of God, and in the Lord's Supper. These are the gifts given in God's holy house, in God's holy name, and in His holy presence for now and for all eternity.

Glossary

Absolution. The announcement of forgiveness to the penitent sinner.

Agnus Dei. Latin for "Lamb of God"; see John 1:29.

Alleluia. Hebrew for "praise the Lord."

altar. A stone or wooden structure at the center of the chancel from which the Lord's Supper is celebrated; the sacramental focus from which God gives His gifts; the sacrificial focus of the congregation's worship.

Apostles' Creed. *See* Creed.

Athanasian Creed. *See* Creed.

Baptism, Holy. Sacrament by which the Holy Spirit creates faith through the application of water connected with God's Word.

Benediction. From the Latin for "[The Lord] bless [you]"; the Aaronic Blessing (Numbers 6:24–26) is commonly used in connection with Holy Communion, while the Apostolic Blessing (2 Corinthians 13:14) is used at other times.

canticle. Latin for "little song"; Scripture texts sung as part of the liturgy.

celebrant. Pastor administering the Lord's Supper.

Church Year. The Church's calendar organized to observe the events in the life of Christ and the Church; sets the theme for each service.

collect. Short prayer.

Communion, Holy. The celebration of Christ's true body and blood under the forms of consecrated bread and wine. Christians eat and drink this Sacrament for the forgiveness of sins and the strengthening of faith; also referred to as the Eucharist, the Lord's Supper, or the Sacrament of the Altar.

Confession (of Sins). The act by which one admits or confesses sin(s) and the guilt of sin.

consecrate. To dedicate to the Lord; to declare holy, as when Jesus' words are spoken over the bread and wine during the celebration of the Lord's Supper.

Creed. From the Latin word *credo*, "I believe"; a summary of what the Church believes; refers to any of the three Ecumenical Creeds used in worship: the Apostles' Creed, often used at Baptisms, funerals, and non-Communion services; the Nicene Creed, often used at services with Holy Communion; and the Athanasian Creed, often spoken on Trinity Sunday.

Divine Service. The name of the regular weekly service that includes the celebration of the Lord's Supper; derived from the German *Gottesdienst*.

doxology. From the Greek for "words of praise"; a short ascription of praise to the triune God: the Father, the Son, and the Holy Spirit.

Epistle. From the Greek word for "letter." In the Divine Service, the Epistle is the second reading, usually drawn from an Epistle in the New Testament.

Eucharist. Greek for "giving thanks"; another name for Holy Communion, the Lord's Supper, or the Sacrament of the Altar; originates from Jesus' giving of thanks over the bread and wine at the institution of this special meal.

Gloria in Excelsis. Latin for "glory in the highest"; the angel's song (Luke 2); a Hymn of Praise in the Divine Service.

Gloria Patri. Latin for "glory to the Father"; a liturgical text used to conclude a psalm or Introit.

God's Word. The Holy Scriptures; the inspired revelation of God's plan and record of salvation.

Gradual. A liturgical response, drawn from the Bible, which follows the Old Testament Reading.

Holy Gospel. A reading from one of the first four books of the New Testament as part of the Service of the Word; always contains the words or deeds of Jesus.

Hosanna. Hebrew word of praise meaning "save us now"; shouted by the people as Jesus entered Jerusalem before the events of Holy Week; included in the Sanctus.

hymn. Song of prayer or praise in stanza form.

Hymn of the Day. Chief hymn of the Divine Service; a hymn specifically selected to reflect the theme of the day, especially the Holy Gospel.

Introit. Latin for "enter"; psalm verses sung or spoken at the beginning of the Divine Service.

Invocation. From the Latin for "call upon"; the words "In the name of the Father and of the Son and of the Holy Spirit" spoken at the beginning of the service; serves as a reminder of Holy Baptism.

Kyrie eleison. Greek for "Lord, have mercy." The Kyrie is the first prayer of the congregation in the Divine Service; it is a cry for mercy that our Lord and King hear us and help us in our needs and troubles.

Lord's Supper. Another name for Holy Communion, the Sacrament of the Altar, or the Eucharist.

Nunc Dimittis. Latin for "now let [your servant] depart"; Simeon's Song (Luke 2:29–32); the Post-Communion Canticle after the distribution of the Lord's Supper.

Offering. The gathered gifts that God's people present in gratitude to the Lord during the Divine Service.

Offertory. Biblical text usually sung as the offering is received at the altar.

Ordinary. Parts of the service that remain the same each week, for example, the Kyrie and the Sanctus.

pastor. Latin for "shepherd"; the title for the congregation's public minister who is ordained and called to be the spiritual supervisor of the "flock" that gathers around Word and Sacrament to receive God's good gifts.

Pax Domini. Latin for "the peace of the Lord"; spoken by the pastor as he holds the body and the blood of Jesus before the congregation.

pericope. Greek for "section"; the portion of Holy Scripture appointed to be read on a given Sunday or festival day in the Church Year.

Prayer of the Church. The longest prayer of the Divine Service; takes up the needs of the world, the Church, the congregation, and local and special concerns.

Preface. Proclamation of praise and thanksgiving that begins the Service of the Sacrament; concludes with the Proper Preface, which changes according to the Sunday, festival, or season of the Church Year.

Propers. Parts of the service that change according to the Sunday or festival of the Church Year, for example, the Introit and the Scripture readings.

rubrics. Latin for "red"; instructions for the minister(s) and congregation concerning how to conduct a service; often printed in red.

Sacrament. From the Greek word "mystery"; a sacred act instituted by God in which God Himself has joined His Word of promise to a visible element and by which He offers, gives, and seals the forgiveness of sins earned by Christ; Holy Baptism and Holy Communion.

Sacrament of the Altar. Sacrament by which the Lord offers His body and blood under the form of consecrated bread and wine for Christians to eat and drink; through such eating and drinking, communicants receive the gifts of the forgiveness of sins and the strengthening of faith; also called Holy Communion, the Eucharist, and the Lord's Supper.

Salutation. Special greeting between pastor and people: "The Lord be with you," followed by the response "And also with you" or "And with your spirit."

Sanctus. Latin for "holy"; follows the Preface in the Service of the Sacrament; based on Isaiah 6:3 and Matthew 21:9.

Sermon. Latin for "speech"; the pastor's proclamation of Law and Gospel based on the Scripture readings appointed for a particular Sunday or festival day in the Church Year.

Service of the Sacrament. Second main part of the Divine Service, beginning with the Preface.

Service of the Word. First main part of the Divine Service, beginning with the Introit.

"This Is the Feast." A Hymn of Praise; often used as an alternate to the Gloria in Excelsis for festival days in the Church Year and the Easter season because of its strong resurrection theme.

Trinity, triune. One true God in three persons: Father, Son, and Holy Spirit.

Verba Domini. Latin for "the words of the Lord"; *see* Words of Our Lord.

Verse. A response sung between the Epistle and the Gospel readings in the Divine Service.

Words of Our Lord. The words spoken by Christ when He instituted the Sacrament of the Altar (Matthew 26:26–28; Mark 14:22–24; Luke 22:19–20; 1 Corinthians 11:23–25); the pastor speaks these very words of Christ in the Service of the Sacrament at the consecration of the bread and wine.

worship. The service to which God calls and gathers His people to give to them the gifts of life and salvation by means of Word and Sacrament.

On entering a church

Lord, I love the habitation of Your house and the place where Your glory dwells. In the multitude of Your tender mercies, prepare my heart that I may enter Your house to worship and confess Your holy name; through Jesus Christ, my God and Lord. Amen.

Before worship

O Lord, my Creator, Redeemer, and Comforter, as I come to worship You in spirit and in truth, I humbly pray that You would open my heart to the preaching of Your Word so that I may repent of my sins, believe in Jesus Christ as my only Savior, and grow in grace and holiness. Hear me for the sake of His name. Amen.

After worship

Almighty and merciful God, I have again worshiped in Your presence and received both forgiveness for my many sins and the assurance of Your love in Jesus Christ. I thank You for this undeserved grace and ask You to keep me in faith until, with all Your saints, I inherit eternal salvation; through Jesus Christ, my Lord. Amen.

Prayers

Before Confession and Absolution

Almighty, everlasting God, for my many sins I justly deserve eternal condemnation. In Your mercy You sent Your dear Son, my Lord Jesus Christ, who won for me forgiveness of sins and everlasting salvation. Grant me a true confession that, dead to sin, I may be raised up by Your life-giving absolution. Grant me Your Holy Spirit that I may be ever watchful and live a true and godly life in Your service; through Jesus Christ, my Lord. Amen.

Before communing

Dear Savior, at Your gracious invitation I come to Your Table to eat and drink Your holy body and blood. Let me find favor in Your eyes to receive this Holy Sacrament in faith for the salvation of my soul and to the glory of Your holy name; for You live and reign with the Father and the Holy Spirit, one God, now and forever. Amen.

Thanksgiving after receiving the Sacrament

Almighty and everlasting God, I thank and praise You for feeding me the life-giving body and blood of Your beloved Son, Jesus Christ. Send Your Holy Spirit that, having with my mouth received the Holy Sacrament, I may by faith obtain and eternally enjoy Your divine grace, the forgiveness of sins, unity with Christ, and life eternal; through Jesus Christ, my Lord. Amen.